Hello!
I am a giraffe.

I0108774

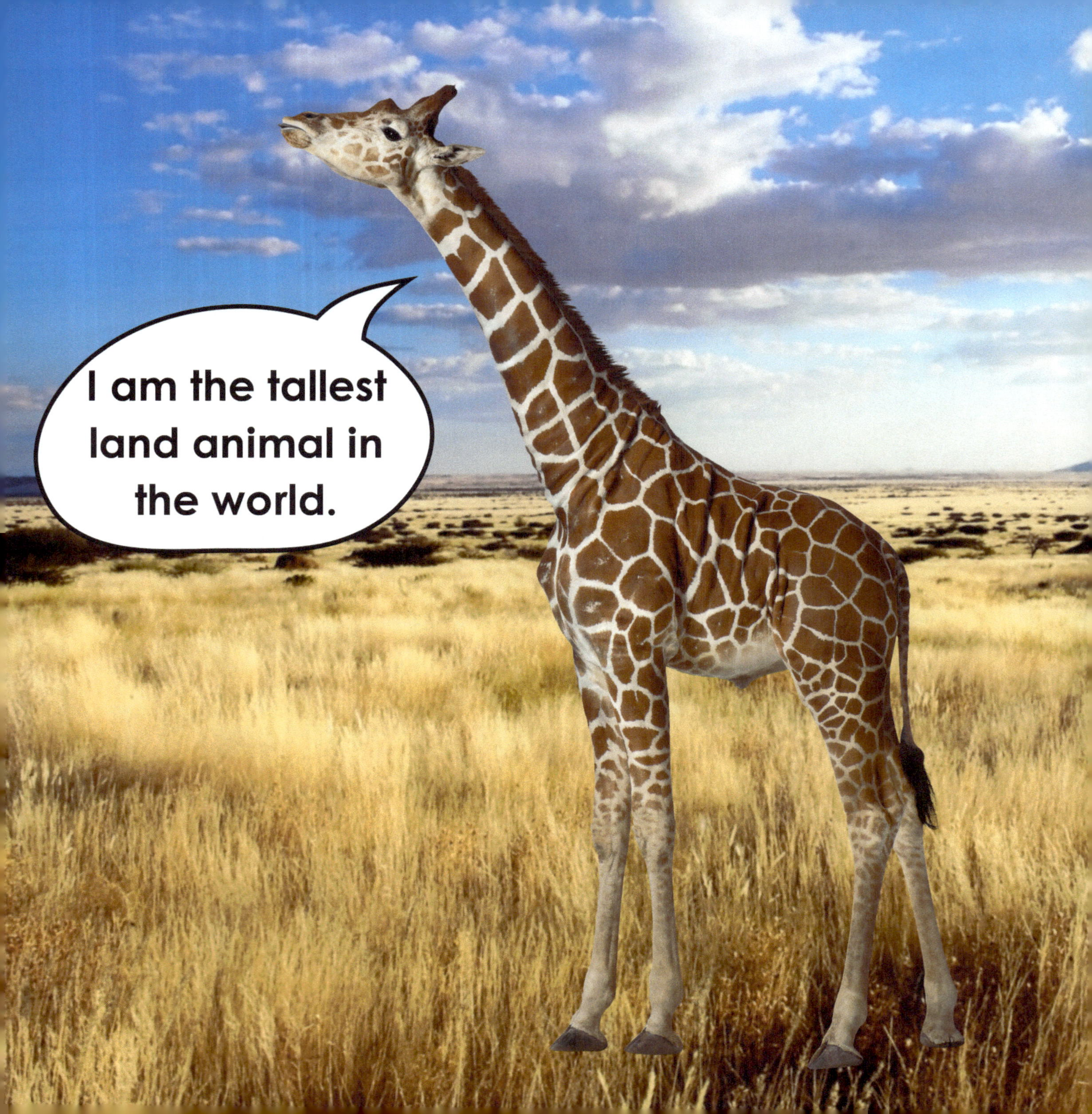
I am the tallest land animal in the world.

The giraffe's long neck is too short to reach the ground.

So, they have to
bend their knees...

...or stretch their legs wide to get a drink.

Giraffes can survive 2-3 days without drinking water.

I have a super long tongue.

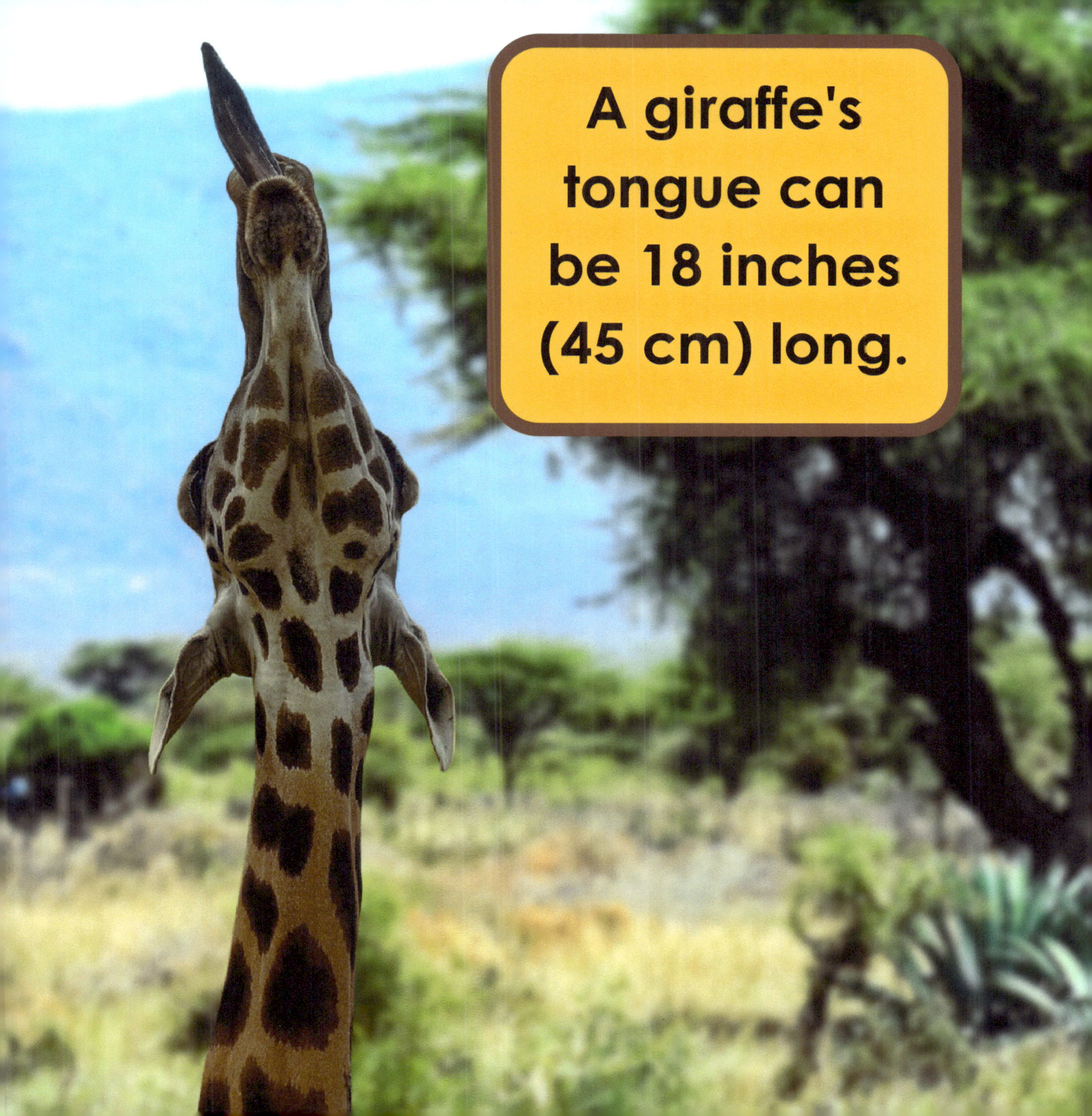

A giraffe's tongue can be 18 inches (45 cm) long.

I am a herbivore.

A "herbivore" is an animal that only eats plants.

I enjoy munching on leaves, twigs and fruits.

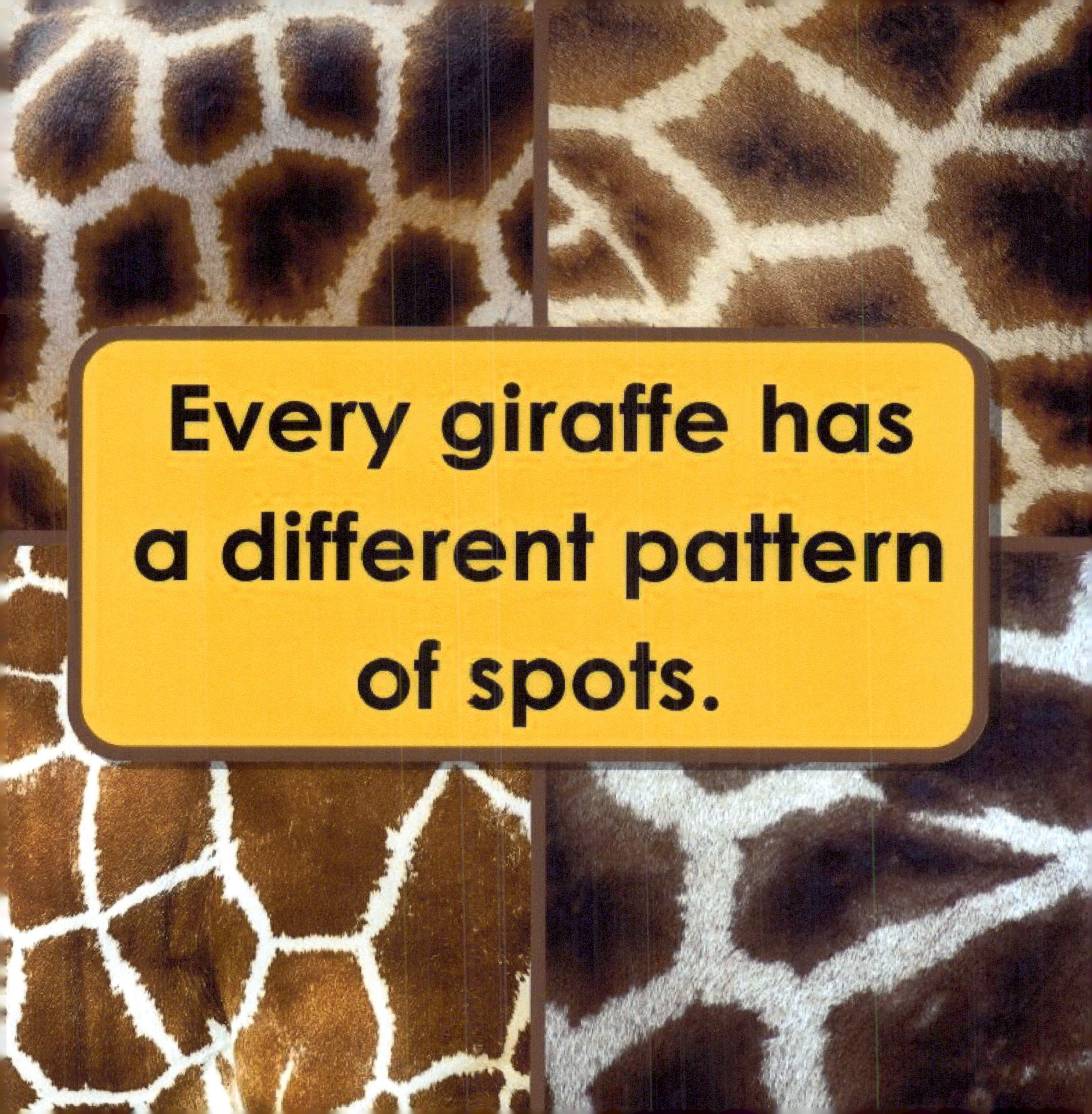

Every giraffe has a different pattern of spots.

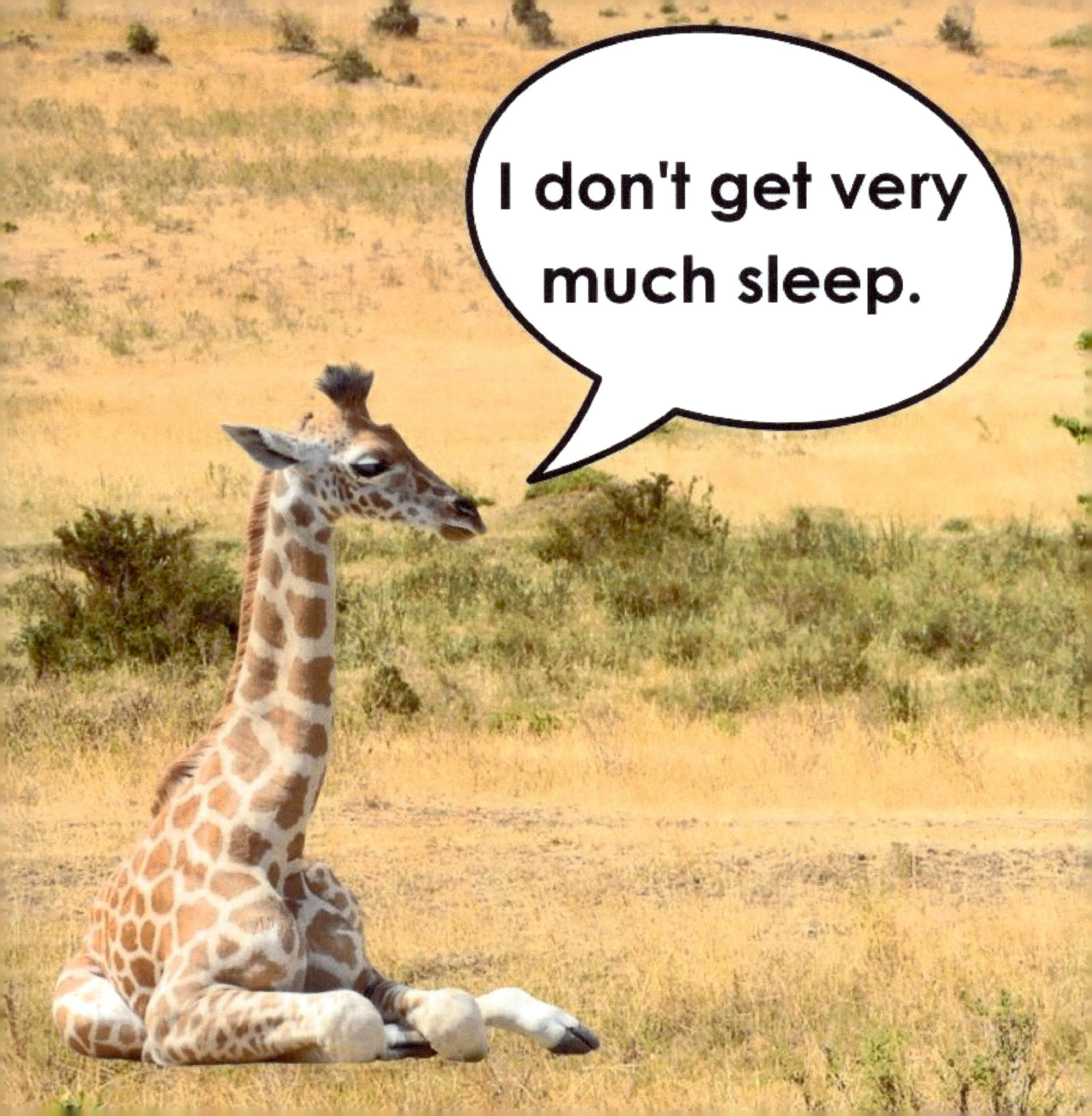
I don't get very much sleep.

Giraffes only sleep for about 30 minutes to 2 hours a day!

Giraffes communicate with each other by making low humming sounds.

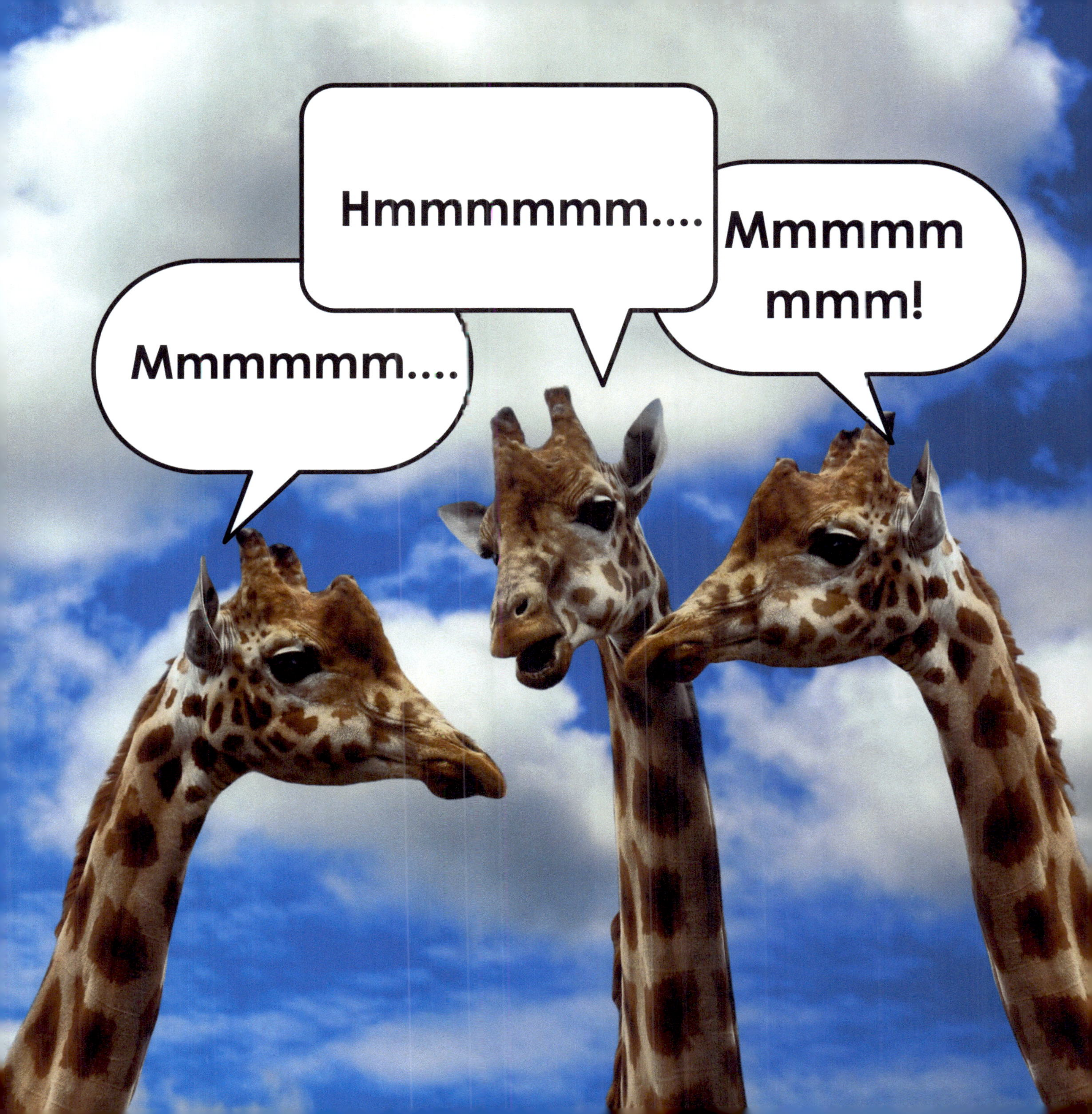
Mmmmmm....
Hmmmmmm....
Mmmmm
mmm!

Giraffes also use body language, like neck swinging and headbutting.

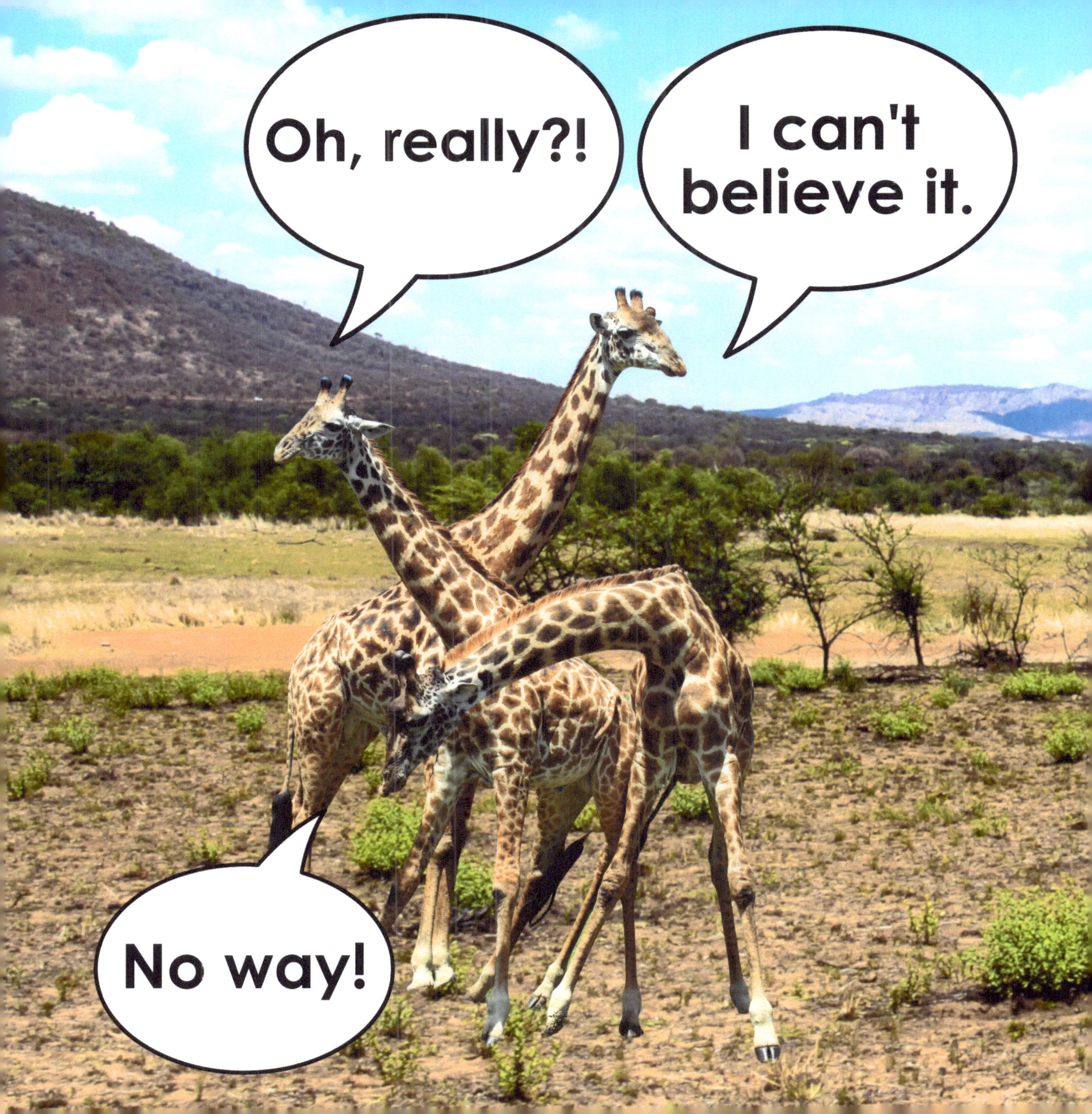
Oh, really?!
I can't believe it.
No way!

A group of giraffes is called a "tower".

They often stay together for protection and friendship.

Giraffe's have **4 stomachs,** just like cows.

Giraffes have a great sense of hearing and smell. It helps them find predators like lions.

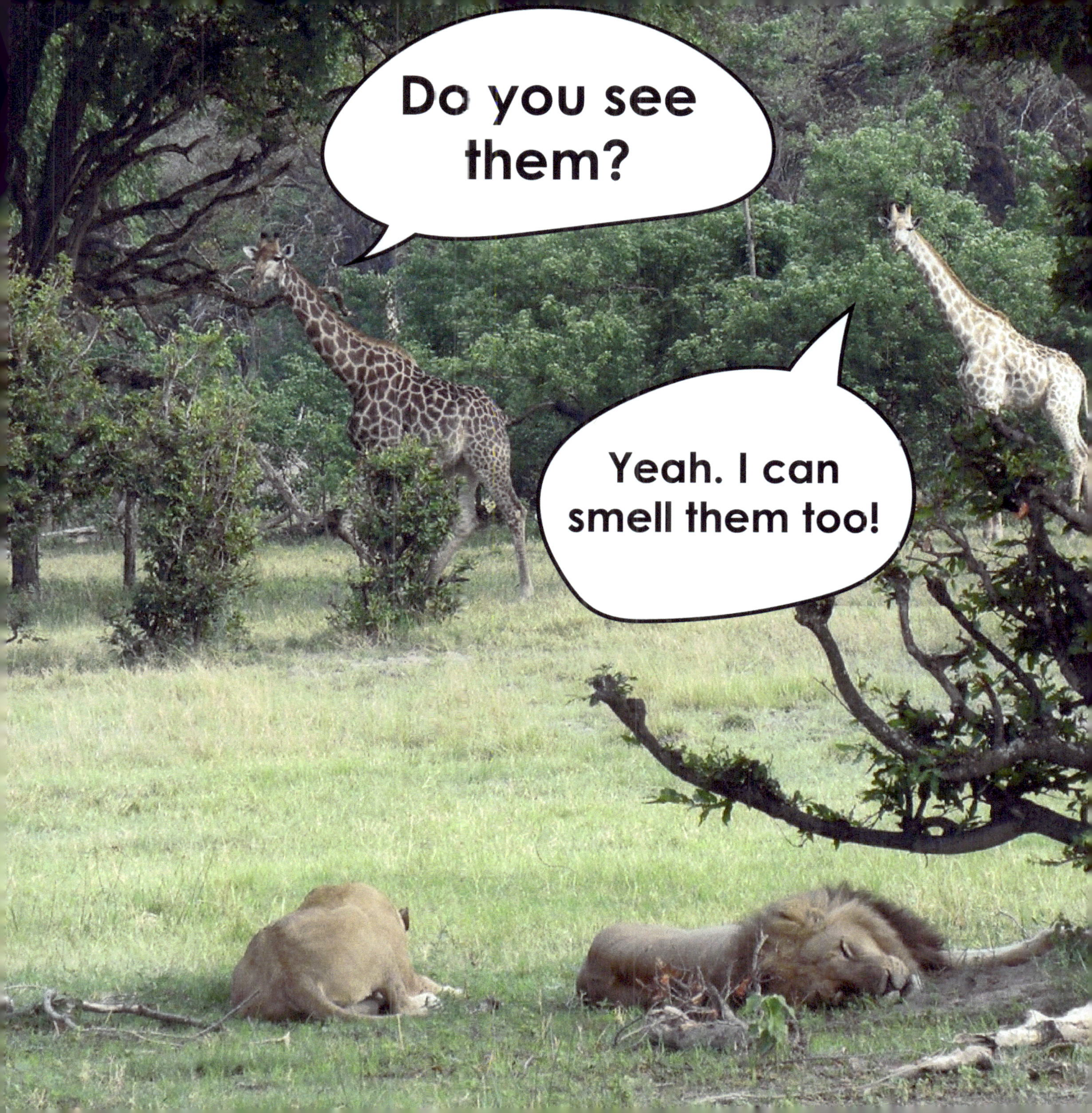
Do you see them?
Yeah. I can smell them too!

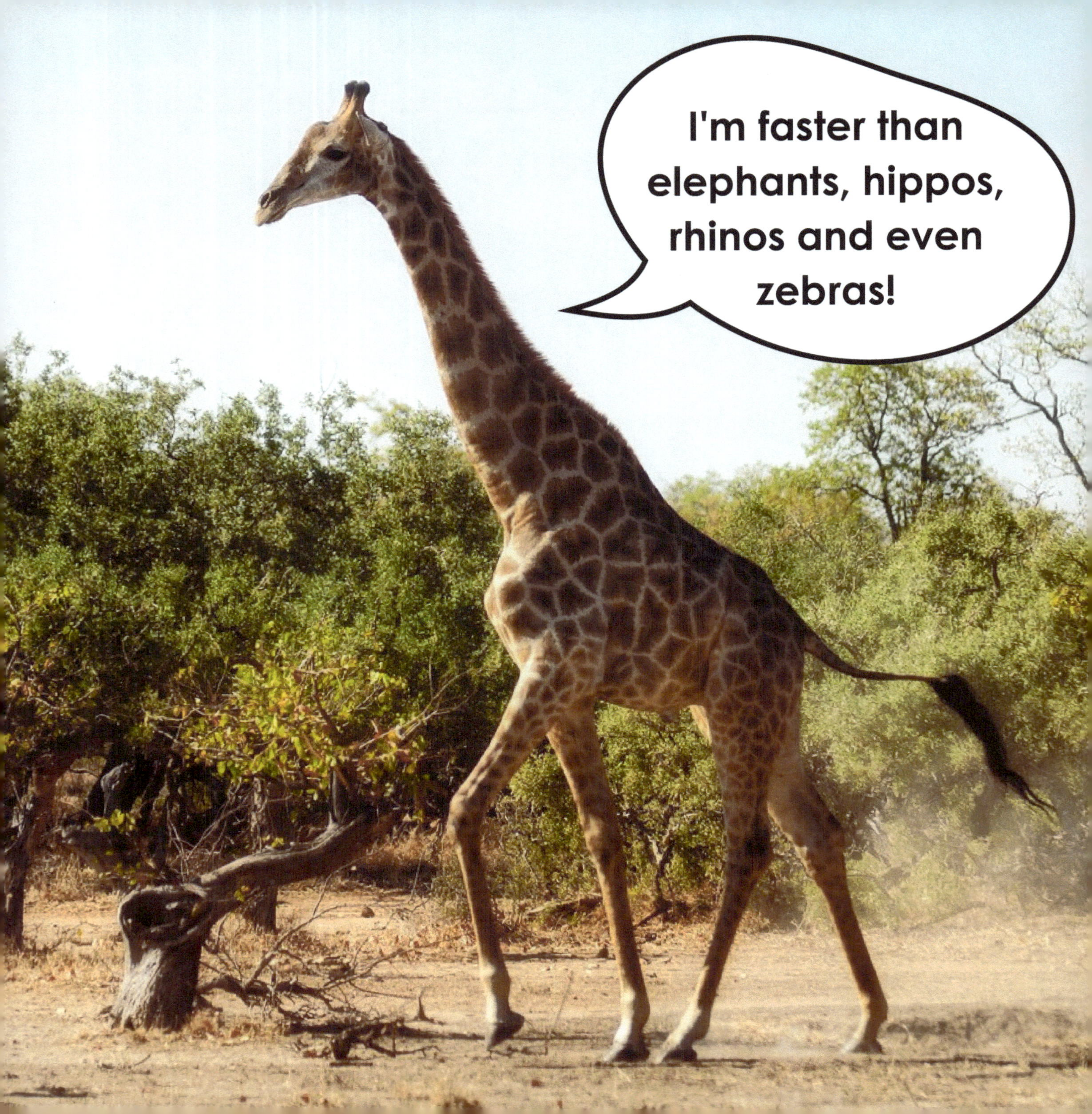
I'm faster than elephants, hippos, rhinos and even zebras!

A giraffe can run up to 35 miles (55 km) per hour.

A giraffe's heart beats
170 times per minute!

Baby giraffes can start walking just one hour after being born.

Hello parents!

Visit us to find out about new releases and **FREE** offers. We'll let you know when we have a new release coming out and how you can get it for FREE.

And you can cast your vote for what book we make next!

scan here

ActiveBrainsBooks.com

or visit here

---

scan here

Let us know what you think. As an independent publisher, your honest reviews mean a lot to us and our business. We'd love to hear from you!

or visit here

amazon.com/review/create-review/

FOLLOW US on Amazon.

amazon.com/author/activebrainsbooks

ActiveBrainsBooks.com

ACTIVE BRAINS

www.ingramcontent.com/pod-product-compliance
Lightning Source LLC
Chambersburg PA
CBHW042057040426
42447CB00003B/252